Reservation Life Today

THIS EDITION

Editorial Management by Oriel Square
Produced for DK by WonderLab Group LLC
Jennifer Emmett, Erica Green, Kate Hale, *Founders*

Editor Maya Myers; **Photography Editor** Nicole DiMella; **Managing Editor** Rachel Houghton;
Designers Project Design Company; **Researcher** Michelle Harris; **Copy Editor** Lori Merritt; **Indexer** Connie Binder;
Proofreader Susan K. Hom; **Authenticity Reader** Dr. Naomi R. Caldwell; **Series Reading Specialist** Dr. Jennifer Albro;
Navajo Consultants Elisabeth Burbank, Danielle Burbank; **Ojibwe Consultant** Madeline Treuer,
Gaa-waabaabiganikaag, White Earth Band of Ojibwe; **Seminole Consultants** Matthew Griffin, Pedro Zepeda;
Yakama Consultants Michael Buck, Keegan Livermore, Blake Slonecker, Priscilla Jayann Arty Thomas

First American Edition, 2024
Published in the United States by DK Publishing, a division of Penguin Random House LLC
1745 Broadway, 20th Floor, New York, NY 10019

Copyright © 2024 Dorling Kindersley Limited
24 25 26 27 10 9 8 7 6 5 4 3 2 1
001–339786–Sep/2024

All rights reserved.
Without limiting the rights under the copyright reserved above, no part of this publication may be reproduced, stored in or introduced into a retrieval system, or transmitted, in any form, or by any means (electronic, mechanical, photocopying, recording, or otherwise), without the prior written permission of the copyright owner.
Published in Great Britain by Dorling Kindersley Limited

A catalog record for this book is available from the Library of Congress.
HC ISBN: 978-0-7440-9442-8
PB ISBN: 978-0-7440-9441-1

DK books are available at special discounts when purchased in bulk for sales promotions, premiums, fund-raising, or educational use. For details, contact:
DK Publishing Special Markets, 1745 Broadway, 20th Floor, New York, NY 10019
SpecialSales@dk.com

Printed and bound in China

The publisher would like to thank the following for their kind permission to reproduce their images:
a=above; c=center; b=below; l=left; r=right; t=top; b/g=background

123RF.com: czalewski 20-21t; **Alamy Stock Photo:** AP Photo / Jim Mone 16-17, AP Photo / Luis M. Alvarez 20cra, AP Photo / Rick Bowmer 41tl, AP Photo / Yakima Herald-Republic, Gordon King 45br, Associated Press / Evan Abell / Yakima Herald-Republic 37br, Associated Press / Mason Trinca / Yakima Herald-Republic 36cra, Keith Crowley 15tl, DanitaDelimont.com 6-7b, David R. Frazier Photolibrary, Inc. 40br, Jeffrey Isaac Greenberg 17+ 26, 44br, Jeffrey Isaac Greenberg 5+ 23crb, Jeffrey Isaac Greenberg 7+ 25br, IanDagnall Computing 37tr, imac 15bl, Imagebroker / Arco / TUNS 45bl, Ilene MacDonald 12cra, M. Timothy O'Keefe 24-25, George Ostertag 38, REDA &CO srl / Riccardo Lombardo 8br, Todd Strand 14b, Chijo Takeda 40-41, Joel Zatz 21crb; **Bridgeman Images:** 39tr; **Dreamstime.com:** Dpimborough 16cra, Andrei Dubadzel 18crb, Helgaknut 28-29t, Mtilghma 22-23, Diane Picard 12-13t, Pictureguy66 13br, Gary Quay 42-43b, Stefan Rotter 19, Stefan Schug 39crb, Josemaria Toscano 39tc; **Getty Images:** Zak Bennett / AFP 22c, Corbis Documentary / Natalie Fobes 40bc, Sylvain Grandadam / Gamma-Rapho 33br, Photodisc / Secret Sea Visions 34br, Richard Lautens / Toronto Star 44bl, Brian Cassella / Chicago Tribune / Tribune News Service 18b; **Getty Images / iStock:** E+ / grandriver 3, 4-5, E+ / Hoptocopter 1, 35, E+ / jimkruger 36br, E+ / THEPALMER 32, 34b, grandriver 28cra, Samson1976 44-45, storkalex 11br; **Library of Congress, Washington, D.C.:** LC-DIG-ppmsc-02526 / Grabill, John C. H., photographer 10, LC-DIG-ppmsca-10050 / O'Sullivan, Timothy H., 1840-1882, photographer 9tr; **Paul Middlestaedt:** 17crb; **Nativestock.com:** Marilyn Angel Wynn 27; **Shutterstock.com:** Darcy Jardine 30-31, Irina Sevostyanova 36-37t; **University of New Mexico Press:** From Earth is My Mother, Sky is My Father by Trudy Griffin-Pierce. Copyright (c) 1992 Trudy Griffin-Pierce, University of New Mexico Press, 1992. 29br; **Courtesy Dr. Donald K Warne, Center for Indigenous Health at Johns Hopkins University:** 9b; **Yakima Herald-Republic:** Sofia Jaramillo 43br

Cover images: *Front:* **Alamy Stock Photo:** ClassicStock / J NETTIS bl, George Ostertag br; **Getty Images / iStock:** E+ / grandriver (background), E+ / RichVintage cl, Juanmonino cr; *Back:* **Getty Images / iStock:** grandriver cra

All other images © Dorling Kindersley Limited
For more information see: www.dkimages.com

www.dk.com

This book was made with Forest Stewardship Council™ certified paper – one small step in DK's commitment to a sustainable future.
Learn more at
www.dk.com/uk/information/sustainability

Publisher's note: Different words can be used for groups of people who are indigenous to a place.
This series uses terms preferred by members of the group being discussed.

Reservation Life Today

Jim Kristofic

Contents

6 Explorers of New Worlds

8 What Is a Reservation?

10 Why Do Reservations Exist?

12	Ojibwe
20	Seminole
28	Navajo
36	Yakama
44	The Exploration Continues
46	Glossary
47	Index
48	Quiz

Explorers of New Worlds

Native Americans know the world through their storytelling. In their stories, Native Americans went to new worlds. Some left the sky to come here. Some came out of the earth. And some traveled through many worlds to reach this one.

Long ago, Native Americans bred plants to make vegetables like corn, beans, potatoes, and squash. Today, some harvest rice, build swamp houses, herd sheep, and fish for salmon.

Some of these Native Americans created the largest true democracies on Earth. They taught people to make decisions that would affect future generations.

There are many differences among Native American peoples. But they also have something in common. Some live on areas of land called reservations. And none of them chose to live there.

What Is a Reservation?

For thousands of years, Native Americans created strong civilizations. They lived across the continent that is now called North America. When people from Europe came to this continent, they brought diseases that wiped out entire populations of Native Americans. The Europeans fought wars against the people who survived. They violently removed Native Americans from most of their lands.

The American Government thought Native Americans should live in separate places from the newcomers from other continents. Reservation land was set aside as a place for Native Americans to farm, hunt, and live.

Reservation Location
Some Native Americans live on reservations far from where they lived before. Other people, like the Hopi, live on reservations where their people have stayed for thousands of years.

The US is a big country made up of 50 states. But inside those states are 324 reservations. They are like small countries inside a big country. Most of their borders were made by the US Government in the 1800s. More than a million Native Americans still live in these small countries today. And millions more visit regularly to connect with their families and the land.

Corn drying in a tree near a Navajo settlement in New Mexico, 1873

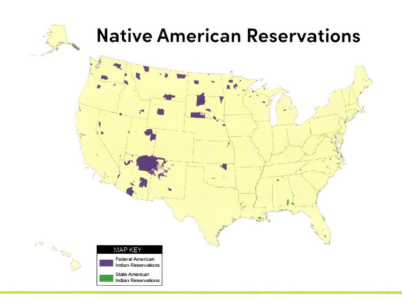

Native American Reservations

MAP KEY
Federal American Indian Reservations
State American Indian Reservations

Why Do Reservations Exist?

Reservations were made in different ways. Some were made by laws written in the US Congress. Some were made by a direct order from the US president.

Some people wanted to move Native Americans off their own land. Settlers and ranchers wanted to use the land for farming and grazing animals. Other people thought reservations would protect Native Americans from being killed by the people who wanted to steal their land.

A group of Miniconjou on the Pine Ridge Reservation, South Dakota, 1890

Some people thought reservations would be temporary. They thought that, over time, all the Native Americans on the reservations would die off. People called them a "vanishing race."

But they did not vanish. They are still here. And they are keeping their traditions alive on their reservations.

Life on each reservation is different, just like life in every country is different. By visiting four reservations, we can learn about different traditions. We'll see what life in some of these small countries can be like today.

All Shapes and Sizes

Some reservations are small, like the Havasupai Indian Reservation at the bottom of the Grand Canyon. Only 214 people live there. The mail is brought in on the backs of mules. The Navajo Nation, on the other hand, is larger than the whole country of Ireland. About 170,000 people live there full time. Many more return regularly.

Ojibwe

Boozhoo! [boo-zhoh] Welcome to the White Earth Nation. We are Anishinaabe [ah-nish-ih-nah-BEH], Ojibwe [oh-jib-WAY], people. We like to dance and move through the seasons in our land of forests and lakes.

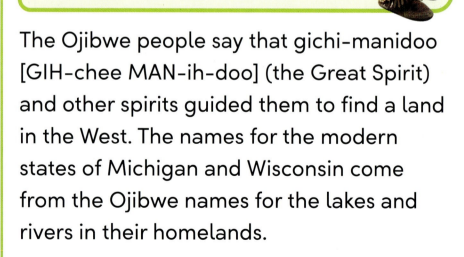

The Ojibwe people say that gichi-manidoo [GIH-chee MAN-ih-doo] (the Great Spirit) and other spirits guided them to find a land in the West. The names for the modern states of Michigan and Wisconsin come from the Ojibwe names for the lakes and rivers in their homelands.

In the 1700s, the Ojibwe became one of the largest tribes in North America. When US President Andrew Jackson signed the Indian Removal Act of 1830, many were forced to leave their lands. Jackson's act was illegal, but only some Ojibwe knew this. The president and the army pushed most Ojibwe to a place they called Indian Territory in Oklahoma. Some Ojibwe were able to keep small pieces of land in Michigan, Minnesota, and Wisconsin.

The Ojibwe believed the Americans were cheating them out of their lands. And they were.

Ojibwe moved with the seasons. In the forests between lakes, they built frames for their wiigiwaaman [wee-gee-WAH-mun]. They covered these frames with reeds or birch bark. When the season changed, they moved their shelter to a frame in a new place. They lived in families, or clans.

Today, Ojibwe people live in modern houses and mobile homes. But every Ojibwe still belongs to a clan. A person's father determines what clan the person belongs to.

"Powwows are ceremonies for healing and celebration. Apart from the spectacle, it's really the culmination of time put into regalia, healing, cultural identity. It's like an artists' fair, but it's all combined in identity and cultural significance. They do special powwows for prayer and exposure to the language and exposure to the community and the elders."

—*Madeline Treuer, member of the White Earth Band of Anishinaabe / Ojibwe people*

Each clan is represented by an animal, ododeman [oh-doo-DAY-mahn]. The clan animals help Ojibwe children see traits of the animals in themselves.

Clans meet at powwows to celebrate their culture. They cook foods like wild rice and blueberries. The people wear special clothes. They perform different styles of dance while drum groups play songs.

Ojibwe people work together to collect food from their lands. In early spring, Ojibwe tap maple trees. They collect the sweet maple sap to cook into syrup or sugar. In the autumn, they gather a wild rice called manoomin, which grows in the water. Ojibwe people say manoomin is a sacred plant.

manoomin

The Ojibwe hunt deer, moose, and birds. They use bows and arrows, as well as snares, just as their ancestors did. They fish with spears and nets.

Ojibwe hunt on their lands. They also go to national forests to hunt. The state of Minnesota does not allow most people to fish with nets. But Ojibwe people are allowed to fish with their traditional nets.

For centuries, the Ojibwe moved through their lands in birchbark canoes called wiigwaasi-jiimaan [WEE-gwas-ih-JEE-mun]. They could carry everything they needed to live in these canoes.

To make this kind of canoe, the builder creates a frame of white cedar wood. This makes the canoe float. The builder covers the frame with birch bark. The pieces of bark are sewn together with cords made of spruce roots. The builder weaves a cedar strip along the top edge of the canoe. Boiled pine sap an deer tallow smeared on the edges make the canoe waterproof.

Ojibwe connect to the spirit world through their dreams. They hang hooped webs called bawaajige nagwaagan [bah-wah-jih-GAY nah-GWAH-gun], or dreamcatchers. The dreamcatchers trap bad dreams and keep them from reaching a person. But the small hole at the center allows good dreams to move through. Many Americans have adopted the use of dreamcatchers.

Seminole

Chehuntamo!
[chee-HUN-tah-moh]
Welcome to the Big Cypress Seminole [SEH-mih-nohl] Indian Reservation. We are Seminole people. We grow plants and fish in our land of rivers and swamps.

The Miccosukee [mik-uh-SOO-kee] people hunted in a place we now call Florida. They shared the land with the Muskogee [muss-KOH-gee], who were farmers. The Muskogee called the Miccosukee the siminoli, which means "wild" or "outcast."

Many Reservations
Today, four Seminole groups live on multiple reservations. The Seminole Tribe of Florida, Miccosukee Tribe of Indians of Florida, and Independent Seminoles live in Florida. The Seminole Nation lives around Wewoka, Oklahoma.

These groups adopted enslaved people who had run away from American plantations. Together, these three groups made up what Americans called the Seminole.

From 1816 to 1858, the US Government started wars with the Seminole. The government wanted to sell Seminole land to farmers and plantation owners. The Seminole worked together to survive the wars. These wars cost the US more money than any other war they fought against Native Americans. Many Seminole were forced off their land. But the US did not win these wars. The Seminole never surrendered.

A historian of Seminole descent, teaching about Seminole history

There are eight Seminole clans in Florida: Panther, Bear, Deer, Wind, Bigtown, Bird, Snake, and Otter. Children belong to their mother's clan. Aunts and uncles from their clan help parents to teach and raise their children.

Seminole Independence
When someone speaks in a tribal meeting, they may say, "I am not speaking for the group. I am speaking for me." People share what they know. They say that this is how they were taught.

Seminole children are taught that they are a part of nature. People are just like the trees, the waters, the grass, and the swamps where they live.

Each child is taught to feel that they are part of the tribe. Their clan uncles and aunts help mentor them. Each child is encouraged to think on their own. Every person has a right to make their own decisions. They have a right to go their own way.

Today, some Seminole people live in modern houses made of wood and concrete blocks. But many Seminole people live in traditional houses called chickees. Wooden poles support roofs made from grass and sabal palm leaves. Chickees have no walls, so the breezes can blow through and cool the people.

Many Seminole live in or near wetlands. They often build chickees three feet above the ground. This protects them against rainwater, floods, and snakes. The people store their bedding and blankets on rafters under the eaves of the roof.

chickee

In their chickees and villages, families grind corn. They make sofkee, a soupy drink made of dried and cracked corn. They roast and dry meats: deer, fish, turtle, alligator, and frog.

Seminole families once made clothing from deer hide and natural fibers. In the early 1900s, they developed a style of clothing called Patchwork. They sew together strips of cotton cloth of vibrant colors. The fabric has patterns like diamonds, crawfish, and birds.

The Seminole gather in the spring for the Green Corn Dance. They give thanks to the Breath Maker for another year. They celebrate the new corn harvest. People talk about what they are planning for the year. They talk about how they are going to vote in tribal elections. Families discuss things they have done that have hurt one another. By talking about the hurt, they can heal and bond again.

Seminole people sometimes cook outside. Many backyards have a cook chickee for cooking under. Fires are built to honor the Wheel of Life. The fire burns at the center of four logs. The logs represent the four directions. The fire begins with the log pointing east, where the sun rises.

The Four Directions
Many Native American cultures place great importance on the four directions: north, south, east, and west. These directions often teach about time, place, thinking, and emotions.

Navajo

Yá'át'ééh!
[yah-ah-t-AY]
Welcome to the
Navajo [NA-vuh-ho]
Nation. We are Diné
[di-NEH], Navajo,
people. We like to visit
one another, ride horses,
and laugh in this beautiful land of
deserts, canyons, and mountains.

The Navajo call themselves Diné, the People. They received their language from the diyin dine'é [DEE-yin DIN-eh] (the Great Ones) and from beings like the dólii [DOH-lee] (Bluebird). The Great Ones helped guide the Navajo to where they live. Their lands lie between four sacred mountains in Arizona, Colorado, and New Mexico.

The Navajo learned to weave and grow corn from Pueblo tribes. They watched Spanish colonists who had brought sheep and horses from Mexico. They learned to herd sheep and train horses.

In 1864, the Navajo people were forced to leave their lands. Four years later, they were allowed to return to a reservation on some of their ancestral lands. Today, their reservation is called the Navajo Nation.

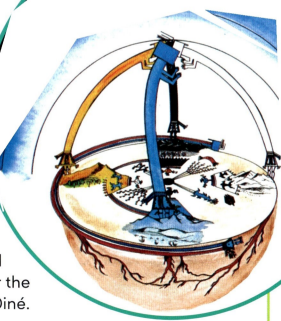

In this painting by Trudy Griffin-Pierce, the sun and moon observe the diyin dine'é (Great Ones) bending from the sacred mountains to watch over the traditional lands of the Diné.

Navajo families organize around women. When a couple marries, they live close to the woman's relatives.

Some Navajo families live on what is called a home site. The tribe gives them a piece of land where they can build a home. The family does not own the land. The land belongs to the entire tribe.

"My grandpa has a horse at Crystal, New Mexico. My grandparents have a hogan at their home site in Crystal. They have a large backyard on the mountain. They have a sweat lodge near the horse corral. My family also does Native American Church ceremonies in a tipi. And Navajo ceremonies when a medicine man comes to the hogan."

—Elisabeth Burbank, age 12, Navajo

At their home site, a Navajo family may build a hogan. A traditional hogan is built with logs and mud. Some modern hogans are built with materials like boards and concrete. Some Navajo families live in modern houses provided by the tribe. These houses are built near places where Navajo people can easily travel to work.

Navajo families often raise sheep, goats, cattle, and horses at their home site. They can graze them on tribal lands. The families often plant corn to make mush, cakes, and bread.

Much of the original Navajo homeland is within their reservation. On the Navajo Nation, families live in small towns, or chapters. In their chapters, Navajo people vote for leaders and laws. They discuss how to bring water to their crops They talk about grazing their sheep and cattle.

Most of the children go to public schools built close to where they live. But some must travel over long stretches of desert highway to get to school.

People come together during ceremonies. They pray to the Great Ones to call their attention. The people make offerings of corn pollen. This helps connect the people to the force of life. With these prayers, the people live in a happy and helpful way.

When a person becomes sick or feels troubled, they consult a medicine singer called a hataałii [ha-TAH-lee]. The medicine singer uses medicines made from nature. The singer chants songs to the Great Ones to help the person heal. The singer also creates sand images on the floor of the hogan. The patient sits on these images to call down the Great Ones.

In the mountains, Navajo people hunt deer and elk with modern bows and rifles. Long ago, they hunted these animals by running. Across the Navajo Nation, it is a tradition to go running in the morning before sunrise.

Navajo girls become women through a ceremony called a kinaaldá [kee-naal-DAH]. As part of this ceremony, the young woman learns to run in the morning, grind corn, and cook for her family. Women often have war names, like Adjabah (She Went Far Off to War). They are considered warriors because they protect their families from the great enemies of hunger and disease.

elk / dzee'

Navajo people weave rugs and blankets. They spin the wool from their sheep into yarn. They weave the yarn on a loom in different styles. They say they received the knowledge of weaving from Na'ashjé'ii Asdzą́ą́ [na-ash-JAY-ih as-dz-AAH] (Spider Woman).

Yakama

Shix̱ máytsk̲i!
[shihx MY-tski] Welcome to the Yakama Nation Reservation in Washington State. We are Yakama [YAH-kuh-muh] people, made up of 14 tribes and bands. Our sacred river is Nch'i Wána [nn-CHEE-wah-nuh], which means "the Big River" (the Columbia River). Our sacred mountain is Pahto [PAH-toe] (Mt. Adams). Here, we fish, hunt, dig roots, and gather huckleberries.

For many centuries, the Yakama people moved between their camps along the rivers in what is now called Washington State. They fished for salmon in the clear waters. They went into the forests to hunt deer and elk.

deer / yukwaasíns

In 1806, some Yakama people met a strange group of people. This group was from a place called the United States. They were led by two men, Meriwether Lewis and William Clark. An interpreter named Sacagawea helped the Yakama talk with these men.

For the next 50 years, fur traders and missionaries from the US tried to claim the Yakama's lands as their own. In 1855, the bands of the Yakama made a treaty with the US Government. The bands united under the leader Kamiakin [kuh-MY-uh-kin]. Soon after, they fought the US soldiers to keep their lands. But like hundreds of peoples before them, the Yakama were forced to move to a reservation.

Years ago, Yakama families lived in lodges made of tule [TOO-lee] reeds. Tule kept the lodges cool in the summer and warm in the winter. Then, other tribes brought horses to their lands. The Yakama were able to travel quickly and carry more trade items to their river camps. They used tule to build tepees, a portable kind of shelter. Today, Yakama people use modern building materials.

Yakama Nation Cultural Center, Toppenish, Washington

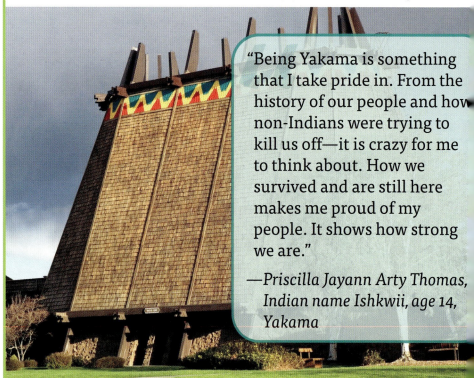

"Being Yakama is something that I take pride in. From the history of our people and how non-Indians were trying to kill us off—it is crazy for me to think about. How we survived and are still here makes me proud of my people. It shows how strong we are."

—Priscilla Jayann Arty Thomas, Indian name Ishkwii, age 14, Yakama

Yakama people moved to river valleys in the winter. In the spring, the snow melted in the mountains. The men, women, and children followed the growth of the plants up the slopes of the Cascade Mountains. They dug roots. They brought ripe huckleberries back to their river villages.

horses / k'úsi

Today, Yakama people fish for Chinook salmon, steelhead, sturgeon, and Pacific lamprey along Nch'i Wána. They climb out onto cliffs along the rivers to use a dip net called a twaluut'áwas [twah-loo-TAW-ahs]. The 30-foot pole has a net at the far end. The fishers move the nets underwater along the steep banks of the rivers. They also use spears and hooks. They feed their families, share with relatives, and sell their catches to local markets.

Yakama children still take time during the school year to harvest huckleberries, dig roots, and hunt.

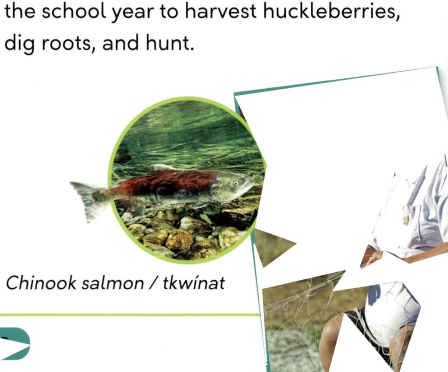

Chinook salmon / tkwínat

The Yakama today have over 10,000 registered members. People from 14 different bands in central Washington State unite under the Yakama tribal council. Their lands cover 1.2 million acres along the Yakima River—but they do not touch the Yakama's sacred river, Nch'i Wána.

The Yakama once lived on lands that covered 12 million acres. That area is almost twice the size of the state of Massachusetts. Today, they live on the Yakama Nation Reservation. This reservation is slightly smaller than the state of Delaware—and 10 times smaller than their original lands.

Columbia River

Some children who live on the Yakama Nation Reservation go to public school. Some attend the Yakama Nation Tribal School. Students can explore and focus on their culture and language, Ichishkíin [ich-ish-KEEN].

Many young people go to the Treaty Day powwow in White Swan, Washington. They dance to heal and connect with each other. They dance to remember the Treaty of 1855. This treaty reserved Yakama rights to fish, hunt, and gather medicine in their original homelands.

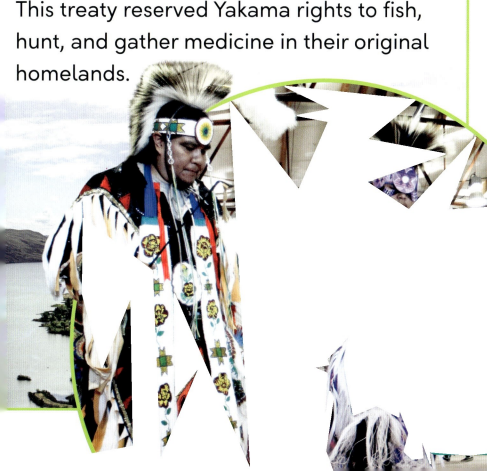

The Exploration Continues

The stories Native Americans tell are still here. The new worlds they explored are still here. The democracies they practiced are still here.

They still teach their children to think for themselves. They remember the wars they fought to keep their lands. They teach others to remember their people.

They have tribal councils. They have schools. They have police and rangers to patrol their lakes. They bring visitors into their swamps. They guide people through their deserts. They care for their rivers.

Native Americans were called a vanishing race. They were put on reservations so they would die off. Now they are leading their nations to live into the future.

Native Americans did not choose to live on reservations. But they choose to be part of life. Reservations are another new world. The people know how to live in new worlds.

Glossary

Ancestor
Someone who lived in an earlier generation of a person's family

Chapter
A small town within a reservation

Clan
A group of related families and individuals

Community
A group of people who live in the same area and share some beliefs and/or cultural practices

Democracy
A government in which the people have power to make decisions

Generation
People who share parents or grandparents; you, your parent, and your grandparent represent three generations of your family

Government
A group that makes and enforces laws

Harvest
To collect a crop of plants

Home site
A place where a family can build a home on tribal land

Homeland
The area or areas where a people feel connected to the place

Interpreter
A person who translates different languages for others to understand

Loom
A frame with strings used to weave fibers into cloth

Medicine singer
A traditional healer who uses plants, animal parts, sand paintings, and songs to help heal

Mentor
To share knowledge and teach important skills

Powwow
A Native American ceremony involving dancing in costume, drumming, and healing prayers

Pueblo tribe
A group of Native Americans who live in a central village made from mud, wood, and stone

Reservation
Land where Native American tribes were forced to live, set aside for their use

Sacred
Held in deep respect and reverence

Traditional
Done in the same way from generation to generation

Tribal council
A governing group made up of representatives elected by members of the tribe(s)

Warrior
A person who develops the strength to protect their people

Index

birchbark canoes 18

Burbank, Elisabeth 30

canoes 18

ceremonies 15, 30, 33, 34

children 23, 32, 43

clans 14–15, 22–23

Clark, William 37

clothing 25

dreamcatchers 19

enslaved people 21

fishing 17, 36, 40

foods and cooking
    Navajo 9, 29, 31, 34
    Ojibwe 15–17
    Seminole 25, 27
    Yakama 36, 39, 40

Griffin-Pierce, Trudy 29

homes 14, 24, 31, 38

Hopi 8

hunting 17, 34, 36

Indian Removal Act (1830) 13

Jackson, Andrew 13

Lewis, Meriwether 37

map 9

Miccosukee 20

Miniconjou 10

Muskogee 20

Navajo 28–35
    ceremonies 30, 33, 34
    families 30–31
    foods and cooking 9, 29, 31, 34
    grazing animals 29, 31, 32
    homes 31
    hunting 34
    language 28
    medicine singer 33
    Navajo Nation 11, 28–29, 32
    running 34
    schools 32
    weaving 29, 35

Ojibwe 12–19
    canoes 18
    clans 14–15
    dreamcatchers 19
    foods 15–17
    history 13
    homes 14
    hunting and fishing 17
    language 12

powwows 15, 43

Pueblo tribes 29

reservations
    locations 8–9, 20, 28
    map 9
    what they are 8–9
    why they exist 10–11

Sacagawea 37

schools 32, 43

Seminole 20–27
    clans 22–23
    foods and cooking 25, 27
    Green Corn Dance 26
    history 20–21
    homes 24
    Patchwork clothing 25
    reservations 20
    tribal meetings 22

tepees 38

Thomas, Priscilla Jayann Arty (Ishkwii) 38

Treuer, Madeline 15

weaving 29, 35

Yakama 36–43
    foods and cooking 36, 39, 40
    history 36–37, 43
    homes 38
    hunting and fishing 36, 40
    lands 42
    powwows 43
    sacred places 36
    schools 43

Quiz

Answer the questions to see what you have learned. Check your answers in the key below.

1. When did the US Government force many Native Americans to move onto reservations?

2. What is used to make Ojibwe birchbark canoes waterproof?

3. Which three groups came together to form the Seminole people?

4. What are small towns on the Navajo Nation called?

5. How long is the pole of a Yakama fishing net?

1. During the 1800s 2. Boiled pine sap 3. Miccosukee, Muscogee, and enslaved people who had escaped from plantations 4. Chapters 5. 30 feet